Steven O'Brien was born in 1963. He grew up singing. His Welsh and Irish family were all conjurers of song. His primal poetic touchstones are the towering hymns of Wales and the muscular ballads of Ireland.

He lives in Worthing and lectures in creative writing at the University of Portsmouth.

His poems have appeared in *Agenda* and in *The London Magazine*. This is his first full-length collection.

STEVEN O'BRIEN

DARK HILL DREAMS

AGENDA EDITIONS

To Stephanie, who loves me because I lick stones

© Steven O'Brien
2006

ISBN - 0-902400-79-7

First published in 2006 by Agenda Editions,
The Wheelwrights, Fletching Street,
Mayfield, East Sussex TN20 6TL
England

Agenda Editions

CONTENTS

War Baby   7

In the Blackout   9
Dark Dregs   11
War Baby   12
Natural Child   13
Hidden Child   14
Baby-sitting   16
Dark Hill Dream   17
Cut-out Memory   19

Hear My Song   21

Inis Mór   23
I Sing the Raparee   24
Welsh Cutlery   26
A Rebel Song   28
Joseph Locke   30
The Bride of Kilcar   32
Singing for Themselves   36

The End of Days   39

Saturday Lash   41
The End of Days   42

Infant Trash   46
Mother Love   48
Hand to Hand   49
Making a Guy   50
1978   52
New Amusements   53
Staring Me Out   55
Santiago   57

Marchland   59

Marchland   61
Cycling the Beast   62
I Will Not Pity   63
To the Sea   65
Shaman Song   67
The Breaking of Him   69

Sea Glass   71

Night Swimming   73
Path of Glass   74
Shoreline Pompeii   75
Sea Glass   76
Linen   77
Budapest – Fin de Siècle   78

War Baby

In the Black Out

Get a swallow down you.
Snatch it quick and sod them all.
Slap a smile across your mouth
And hope the flying masonry
Don't rip it from your face.

A slide of Glen Miller dishing the brass.
Bottles of brown, like loose grenades
Swing his greatcoat pockets.
Oh Johnny oh Johnny how you can love

Her red nails, tacky with brick dust
Grab his lapels,
Curtaining out the black-out alley.
His young hips are iron.
The juice of *In the Mood* lures her belly skywards.

A husband gone faceless after two years away.
Lipless, touchless and voiceless
In scant censored letters.

And this hot now.

A grabbed moment.
Opening in a fuss of serge and buttons.
To have it all now
In unrationed clinching against the wall.

. . . oh Johnny oh Johnny heaven's above

The back gate slams.
Sugar he slushes in her ear
Cutting under the low gut murmur
Of a Dornier overhead.

Dark Dregs

Your mother brewed you from dark dregs –

A sweet pull of cheat,
Shared round the back.

Black market treacle
Running down her leg.

A quick swig of panic
As she tried to ignore your spasms.

A choking half bottle
Of back sniffed tears
And a scalding bath
When she tried to flush you from her.

Then the glass shard pain of you
As you were sluiced into the morning after,
Already broken.
Cast too soon into a bombed out world.

War Baby

You gathered the nub of yourself in a lurching womb
Knocked up,
Pounded at dawn and at midnight
By the black back slosh of hangovers
And bomb thuds.
A to and fro tide
Washing you each night with an early lock-in,
So that you drank the sudden fear
Of the pang that was you.

Natural Child

You were the *natural child.*
A green eyed
Dark thorn changeling.

A bombsite bramble,
Bundled in the dirty linen
Of your mother's worst kept secret.

The wind among the thistles
Was grey
And sounded like disgrace.

It filled your mind with hissing.

Hidden Child

Your hidden girlhood
Was locked away inside you.
Upstairs,
In a house,
In a terrace
Where no one had gone.

It rocked and rocked and rocked,
Moaning at the cot gate.
Drawing you
Down your own unlit streets.

Slip the catch,
No one knows you are here.

And up the dark stairs.
Yearning across the landing.
Groping for that sore room
And the hungry pleading.

Open the bottle
The baby must be fed...

You pressed a teat of scathing liquor to your lips,
Crooning as you dulled
With slack drinking –

Now come the tears.

Walking the floor.
Arms swaddling
Around the lonely bundle.

Hushing and cradling
The desolation you craved to soothe,

And the slow slow despair
That you couldn't mother yourself.

Baby-sitting

This was my mother.

Babysitting her
In the long time
Of a three day binge

I caught her chugging down whiskey,
Suckling on a thirst of razors.

Tried to tear it from her.
She sneered a mouth full of fucks
And her nails were at my face.

Whiskey,
Brown blade juice,
Slashed across my cheek.
I punched her,
Hard.
Peeled her fingers off,
For we had fallen
Locked,
Dragged onto her reeking bed.

This was my mother,
And I know what it is to look into the eyes of a demon
At noon.

Dark Hill Dream

I left you
And you are seven years lost
Under the dark hill of my sleeping...

In the dream I was searching for my mother
In a Sunday school,
With infant laughter,
Like small bells
On a primrose morning.

I knew they were all dead –

These nettle-eyed children
Who followed me
Through curtained halls.

I called her,
As dust tingled on blades of sunlight
And across my flimsy echo,
To a table set for tea.

Spiked grins held behind quick hands.
A pretence of play –
The cunning of the dead.

At the bottom of the back stairs
She was lying –
A bag lady, in coats.
They had laced her with daisy chains.

The slow time of whiskey was upon my mother
And although I shook her
Until her head slammed back
She would not wake.

She was saying
In breath sour as rust,
They won't leave me alone . . . They won't leave me alone.

My voice, snuckling through tears,
Was a boy's again
As I tugged her rags.
For I had come to take her home
And knew I had to leave her.

So I fled
But heard their laughter in the walls,
Like silver bells rung far underground.
And her murmur, slack as yolk

. . . They won't leave me alone.

Cut Out Memory

I unfold this bright cut-out memory
Of you in your cut-out morning –
You take a fresh sheet from the clothesline

And stand on a high wall.
The pure logic of flight
Dazzling
Your small girl's eyes.

You look up
Into the white and blue confusion
Of sky and cotton.

You hold the four corners of a cloud
Billowing above you
And yearn for lift.

No matter that you fall.

I feel the tug
Of the right wind
And sense the pure dare
As you step out
Expecting your toes to fall limp beneath you.

Your swift second of being,
When you are all white and blue and sky.

Hear My Song

Inis Mór

That time
We walked through nine curtains of rain
Downhill to Kilronan
And the American Bar,
Where six men sang
In long curls of Irish

And one among them
Like a wrecked Spaniard,
Dark as dreaming under broken water,
As if his eyes were the plain backs of mirrors
Turned inward on a voice

That surfaced in the tune,
And shoaled out along the western sky
On three fingers of red
Between a power of clouds,
Back up the grey stone miles
To the wind blowing across Dun Aenghus
Beyond the nine waves.

I Sing the Rapparee

To walk the purple heather
And hear the west wind cry
To know that's where the Rapparee must die…

from *Ned of the Hills*. Terry Woods

Many Irish songs and stories speak of the ragged outcast
Rapparee; a fallen nobleman of the Gaelic aristocracy, turned
outlaw.

In the eyes-closed ache of the song
He jags in my vision,
Sudden against the skyline.
Hounded youth –
The Rapparee.

I catch the shattered cut of him
As he hares across
The crow-mobbed sodden hillside of the tune.
Russet jacket rags
Flap and part
To show a winter thicket of ribs
And a shot-out heart.

Rapparee –
Fetter bitten, noose-burnt, gallows-fodder.
Behind my eyes you are harried forever.
Over strewn walls
Through shivering streams.
Face to the rain.
Dragoons, moon and musket behind you.

Mangy Renardine.
Prince-outlaw, brought low.
Wild Éamon an Chnoic –

In the cave of my singing,
Always your back to the wall
At the last.
And the pack come for blood.

Distilled dispossessed,
Tear me again
As you are evicted, starved outrun, lynched.

Hang there,
In the ballad,
A gamekeeper's trophy
Bleeding on my tongue.

Welsh Cutlery

Nan
I will never hear again
The cutlery of your words
Polish off a neighbour's reputation –
Their garden, their cooking.

In there.
Quick forks of valleys silver,
Spearing the lamb chops of small sins –
She's as sly as a bag of monkeys.

Chapel sharpened knives.
Far keener than our teaspoons
Of French cinema.
Our salad tongs
Of World music.

He was no bigger than a bar of soap.

You've got proper fat.
Mind you, it suits you.

Jealous,
You took most of the set with you,
Clutched tight,
When we packed you in the dresser
Wrapped in your lace curtains.

But we all got something from the drawer.

I took *She thinks she's mustard ... but she's not.*
And I'll keep it shiny for you Nan,
To slice into a conversation –

Nod
And look long faced and Welsh
At that strumpet up at number eleven.

A Rebel Song

This is dedicated to my grandfather

A raffish stance by the hearth.
One hand behind your back
The other loose.
A parlour pose.

I found one of your songs in my mouth
And looked back thirty Christmas nights
Through it
And saw you.

Small double cuffed-dandy.
Gentleman's gentleman tie pin
And three piece,
Speaking of parties
Seen through cracks in the door.
Fastidious emulation,
Born of much polishing
In the sheen of your shoes.

But the urbanity of a pencil moustache,
Long studied from the cheap seats,
Could not hide the gnawings
In your bantam frame –
Of a wandering childhood.
Of marrow-wet
Famishing.
Of barn sleep,
Of emigration boat.

And the tremor of your voice –
A lofty cultivation of tears
Bore it out.
So that your forte,
Those doggerels,
The maudlin chucking-out time ballads
Made for pub
And back of the charabanc
Were drawn high-strung
And taut.

I found the song
You had given me
Washing drunk in my mouth –
The fossil of suffering
Labelled in the neat
Never-never hand of sentiment.

And I belted the ceiling,
Singing with the rest of them,

But remembered how
Your faded poster stance
And tremulous rendering
Gave tension and dignity
To the pale complexions of heroes
And weeping mothers.

Josef Locke

See him through the crackles
Of an old seventy eight
As the cornet insinuates
And hisses a sly procurer's lisp.

The conductor's knowing smile
Winking back
At our front row grandmothers,
In their first flush gone
Red-dyed Kathleen hush,
As he nods him in;

Hear my song, Violetta.
The charmer,
In a world dry for a bit of charming.

The thrust of his guardsman's chest.
The grand man.
His Derry-Venetian tenor has enough moonlight
To conjure silver on water
And touch them where their husbands never do –

Rough handed men
Demobbing themselves into bed each night.
Who don't call them *macushla*
In a gondola
Somewhere off Galway Bay.

They open to him,
Like the petals of their crushed hankies,
Yearn for his tears
And yes to be taken
To where their hearts will know no pain.

The Bride of Kilcar

My thirty-fifth birthday

Now here's a good one.

Kilcar festival,
Scrubbed up shiny like a bachelor
After a meagre week
In the back of Donegal.
Peaks I had no name for
Tearing sky and sea into triangles
And all water uphill.

A nose to my ear in the dark
As quick as a blown leaf –
The Bride of Kilcar.

She was eighteen,
And mad with the thrill
Of her one road town gone antic.
Draggled veil,
Make-up blotting,
Shivering,
Giddy-breathless from her crowning.

Face alight
For grabbing a stranger
And dance, chance
Or the end of the world.

And would I like to go to a party?

Cartooned ructions of drunk shadows
In the seep of every pub window.
Silhouettes side-sliding,
Going down in the gutter.

A band on a lorry
Thrashing the downpour,
Slinging dustbins of heavy metal at the moon.

Young ones jumping to the pulse
Of their drenched northern fiesta.

I held her off
At half alarmed arm's length
But with a feeling half like luck in me.

Her wedding dress
Was swan's wing,
A sodden tissue
Strewn out from her grip on me
To the flooded kerb
Like she might be washed away
And drag me with her
On a cascade of sly chat and flattery,

And would I like to go to a party

My smile
Was honey slathered across my chin;
Sticky, foolish.
Buttered up in a doorway
By a girl half my age.

Not up for it
Of course,
But running with the thought,
Laughter dripping back down my throat,

To where I saw me and this girl
Chasing through the loose torrent
In a lash of drink
And the glee of misrule.
Her fresh gown of love
Trailing soaked feathers
Up the pelting street.

Come away to the party now

But I'd laughed my face into lamplight
Spilling the scrap iron of my years
Into the full yellow,
And her eyes.

Her laughter never stopped,
But her hanging off me
Broke.
And she fell up the street
Squealing her daftness.

She turned, grinning
And I shouted –
I'll come away to the party

We both got a slice of the joke
But I think it cut me deepest.

Singing for Themselves

On Inis Mór
In the hanging moments
Of inky twilight
Island men
From fields and the sea
Still gather to sing.

Holding hands
They row the singer out from the day
Into the tune
As they sit and sing for themselves.

He pays out the words
Along his drone
Sliding long on the key
A fragile slipping grip,
But then sure
And dipping and rising.
Uncoiling.

Heads bent,
They share the burden
With locked hands,
Used to hard rhythm.

Their ears watch the story unfold.
It touches their frowns with flickers of recognition.
They nod
And press on.
Pacing their fists.
Living the work.

The back-sprung Irish words
As secret as the seam
Of two lovers' bellies
Touching on a hot bed.

For these songs are heavy
With oiled desire.
A thousand times sung.
A thousand times drawn in.

Pangs caught on the hooks of heartbreak.
Lusts of youth,
Time-rowed smooth
By their straining.
They pull.
Singing for themselves.

A moment of breath.
The song is done.
They laugh and slap each other,
As when together they take in a net
Or draw up a boat.

Shy, they are lost
In a tongue of darkness
By the open door.

The singer grins
And they file out,
To grey houses on the rim of the west.
The night promises rain.

The End of Days

Saturday Lash

I was made in the wet sob of a November night,
Just after chucking out time,
As the gulls screamed down the canyon streets
To the end of the pier
And round again
And the sea opened its throat
On the shingly drag
Back from the beach.

I come from where fun was mucking in
And money was fireworks
Primed in the Saturday pockets
Of boys gulping down their manhood –

All pleasure in a pint glass,
Biting it dry
In case someone snatched the good times.

And girls with dog-meat voices
Heckling in the echoes
Between the click click
Of their fierce heels –
Bare pebbled legs
Mocking winter's teeth.

The End of Days

I

Nineteen seventy six
That day they fired the corn stubble
At the end of a summer
With never a kind moment.

My mother's anger
Like a prophet's curse
Writhed and muscled
Like a stranded eel
In the eye of the sun.

And I ran from the house
With a ripe welt singing across my face.

Weeks of heat
Like the smell of horse blankets,
Like a slump of coats
Falling from a hook.

II

To the ruined barn.
A stone elephant,
Marauded, ransacked,
Dropped among thorns.
Its grey arse stoved in –
Given good wallop.
Walls throbbing
And a boiling green
Chundering from its gaping side.

I hid in its belly,
Thriving in,
Parting the snag and snare,
Under two charred rafters
That tusked out over the nettles.
A parch like a glove on my tongue.

A sulk wrapped in brambles.

III

Old tool blades ate at my ankles.
Iron elf bolts,
Earth woken
To decay into flake and blood dust,
Clogging the fierce noon air.

I lay like a thrashed dog,
Loitering without intent
Along the foetid shadows,
Below spine-bowed beams
Picked bare to the open sky,

And I longed for a lolly
To cut my felted thirst.

But all I got
Was a buzzing mouth of blackberries
Like a clutch of headaches,
The sticky witness staining my hands.

In the barn's guts
I slipped
And laid my leg open,
Wallowing on a rusty spike.
Three wounds welling
To my slow astonishment.

IV

As I pedalled home to face the music
Like swimming through sticky water,
With scorched earth behind me,

A great torso of smoke
Rose from the blazing fields.

My knee was a seeping summer pudding.
A steady pulse oozing, jammy, down my shin.

And a black cloud over my head,
Like the toils of God.

Infant Trash

Drink sprung the locks
Of my mother's gaol.

Sent her quietly mourning
Down her empty corridors,
Trying doors, rattling bolts.

Each night
She came back,
As a wakened, baying child,
Flinging the gob-soiled rags
Of her hatred
In our faces

Three, four nights in a row
In this creaking Wendy house
Of stalking slaps
And trundling steps across the ceiling.
Elastic hours of infant trash.

Baby was awake,
Screaming misery,
And ready to claw the eyes from the world.

Long snotty wailing
That put us at the end of a desert
Of ravaged darkness,
Where we rocked for numbness
And crushed the screeching from our ears.

A baby given a woman's body
To tantrum in.

We served for It those nights.
The Great Torturer.
The life breath
She had never asked for.

And she would pay us back,
In filthy protest.
Spite without knowledge.
And flog her own carcass ragged
For the dreadful agony
The world had done.

Mother Love

You have heard the wailing
Of a livid baby,
Leaching colour from the world
And the face of the mother
In thrall
To the infant's pure rage,
As it kicks and screams itself purple
Against some agony
It cannot name.

My mother tended her youngest child,
An elemental of raw need
And jealousy
That would not be comforted.
She bent to it,
Feeling for its pain,
Shutting out our clamour.
Gave herself
With a soundless womb-ache,
Beyond love,
To the never-born within her.

Hand to Hand

I was taught that you give honour to your hand
By making a fist of it.
And never let your head down.

Grandads and great uncles,
Flyweight heroes,
All jaw and tight tie,
Strutting in sepia
Who'd gone to war for brawl and plunder
And one who'd been in gaol for fighting.

That nasty runt James Cagney,
Their idol.
Touchy popinjay –
His hands clumped
Into a pair of itchy hammers.

Respect held cocked,
Spring-loaded in white,
On the studs of their knuckles.

And a smile meant *Come here son.*
Over here.
I've got something for you...

Making a Guy

The dining room was our dark tower
Where we three bent to the task
And did the business.

Shirt, trousers, jumper
Laid out –

The grubby surgery of stolen parts and balled newspaper:
Screwed and torn words stuffing a man's clothes,
Hands smirched with print.

The crumple as we fixed the head,
And sat it up.
Supreme moment of collusion.
Like we had pulled the switch –

He was made.

Settling creaking,
His tilting head and lumpy hunchback
Seemed more his fault than ours.

The back gate swung its rusty mewling.
Dry leaf fingers flicked the window;

O what prickling unchancy thing had we done?

Judas face and clumsy semblance.
Those eyes I'd drawn, you wouldn't turn your back on now.
Four bodies in a room where there had been three.

Three children dragging him down the path.
His slack unhinged limbs
Trailing the cobbles.

And all afternoon we watched him
Akimbo on the pile of rubbish,
To see if he might move.

1978

Punk might have been witty –
Badges, school blazers
And grandad's tie irony,
At the art college.

But in the open mouth
Of the recreation ground,
Broken swings and youth club,
It was just nasty.

Day-glo pink
Bubble gum girls
Fingered rotten
Against the back wall of the bogs
By boy-men
In dog end docs
Ratting up from the estate.

She fucked for cider.

He held a knife to my face.

We gnawed on ourselves.

New Amusements

Astrid, impossibly blonde.
Both of us fourteen.
Me dark and lucky
In the eye of a staring moon.

Worthing pier
A spider's underbelly
Of splayed black gantry
Hanging above us,

Her Lapp-slanted eyes
And upturned nose invisible,
But so close we shared breath.
Her strawberry lipstick
Was how I imagined wine might be.

A xylophone of spare-ribs.
Navel to navel
I traced the Braille of a fancy menu
I could hardly read.

Tiny sherbet lights,
Red and blue
Slinked through the decking.
New Amusement slot machines
Coughed.

And although it was nothing more
Than a hand in each others' shirts,
Touch had tasted the first course –

The great grip hunger
Which had been panging me
Pulled down through my hips
To the slow draw-suck of stones
Below me, below her,
And I was terrified.

I walked a long three miles home
Along a newly shifted beach.
A giant silence ringing in my ears.

Staring Me Out

Worthing in the thinnest rain.
Gulls mourning their empty bellies.
Eating the sky with open shrieking.

I caught my eye
Behind the bar, in a glitter of bottles.
I held my look
Among the optics –
Fixed in the silver

And stared myself out.

Out
On the spattered evening
Over my shoulder.

A gull tore my face away.
Carried it over the pier,
A white rag,
A damp piece of litter,
And dropped it in the dark
Where sky meets water.

My open head,
Hollowing
With sharp gull's cries,
As I watched my limp brow wash up
In the mirror
Amid a mob of drinkers.

Pubs lit yellow
Like empty carriages,
Stretching back
Around the curves of years
To the trundling under-night
Of the last tube home from Kilburn
And the late teen cult of myself.

The first time I sliced into my stare.
I'd drunk my head empty.
Empty.
Apart from a lonely love of my own face.

The window swallowed my infatuation
Out into the black sea between stations
And pitched it back,
White and viscous,
Like a gull had coughed it from its crop.

Santiago

A first glass of Ribiero –
Shiver of green
Over the rim
Of the cold stone bowl.

Bagpipes
Fanning through the rain,
Rising and falling,
Like a mistuned radio.

The night stretching out
From our feet.
Slow understood and right.
A long wet passeo ahead,
In a city made for drinking.

Mejillones, empanada, pulpo;
Small tapas offered obliquely
By grave, impeccable waiters.
A deliberation of wine.

A Cuban dancing salsa alone.
Having his spicy fun straight faced.

Laughter on the stones
Of damp vaulted bars.

Dwelling plundered time.
Quietly squandered.
Bites of talk.

Rain plastering our hair
Until we are two brilliantined grandees
With lids half closed
Eyeing the girls –

And a steady paced descent
Into liquidity.

Rain trickles from my brow
To the lips,
Mingles with the wine.

The Gaitero and his pipes
Always a street away,
As we call at every place
On the Rua Del Franco.

Marchland

Marchland

This marchland.
Neither sea nor land.
Nothing but the wind fumbling
Across a queaze of mud and suck.

Give me your name it says.
Hook it from your gut.

In return
I will hang two shells
To swing under your ribs
And chime, chime.

Looking at you, I consider this fair.

It spreads its arms
And spins on the sand.

I say – I cannot help you

... *Cannot help you* it shouts back.

I turn and climb the shingle.
Sky-high laughter
Gulling over low-tide flats
Cuts like a fish knife.

Cycling the Beast

Cycling this mean uphill
In the mad noon
The tawny scrub twitches
And stinks of hide.
Like riding the flank of a giant bullock.

The stinging road gores the sun.
Yellow salt bleeds in my eyes.
I choke on dry ochres.

I know this climb detests me.
It snorts grit.
Its thighs lock,
As I scale against myself –

Along the limestone spine
That bucks and horns
Out over the canyon side
And bellows red-minded in my ears –

A steer raging for its stolen soul
That leaps forever across a cave roof
In the guts of these hills.

I Will Not Pity

Please don't let me love you
For I know you'll break my heart

Hank Williams.

It is midnight
In the honky tonk of misery.

I will not pity
This white-trash death
You have given yourself,

Although the pink petals
Of your bar-fly glamour
Are crisp and strewn
Along this hospital bed.

I will not kiss your yellow hand
As between the two-step
Beat of the respirator
The smoke of all your husky lies
Brushes past my face.

I cannot bend to those parched lips
Still flickering with the fading rhinestones
Of cheap and fragile fantasies.

The closing treacle slide
Of a lonely country song –

Pines around
The gin-haunted spite
And brawling thirst
That cut me out for twenty years.

And my eyes bite at a fist of tears

... But please don't let me love you
For I know it just can't be.

To the Sea

And now you Karen
You go your way.

Street-lights glaze wet pavements.
I walk on squares of slab-sheen
Placed over the mouth
Of an open grave.

Oval leaves flake ahead of me.
Shedding reflections
Which skate under the path's surface,
Pale as lemon peel in the black –
Like all your fallen faces.

My sister,
Still crumpled like a tissue
In a pink hospital nightie,
On your last bed.

Your fingers gripe in time
To the monitor's bleat.
Your heart is its dance partner,
For a while.
But it does not know the steps.

You will not wake again.

They say your mind has fallen
Into the cold stream
That runs below the glass
Of these November streets.

Now I see
How the wires and drips
Snag your arms like weeds,
And your empty lips fret
In answer to a distant voice.

You are calling your body to swim.
To follow,
To the open sea.

Shaman Song

I have been into the hare.
I laid its long ears flat

And watched the Herd-Lord pass
Dribbling His spunk
On the meadow flowers.

I have been into the bee.
In its round song, its dusts of gold.

I hung above His autumn belling
And lulled the Bull
To rest His raunching thighs.

I have been into the salmon.
In a pulse of stream-sluiced muscle

I leapt to taste His warm breath
As he lowered His horns
And drank the moonlit shallows.

I have been into the cat.
In its silver hiss and snarl.

The first snow flecking
The forest edge
I crouched and stared yellow
Under the shadow of His rutting.

The Breaking of Him

Men did manage to hold out against the manacles – and
Guido was nothing if not strong – but against the rack never.

Antonia Fraser – *The Gunpowder Plot*

Fawkes

His first signature brags –
Second-hand Spanish manners,
Polished and flashy –
Across the parchment.

Listen.
In the before and after
Between arrest and admission
Stretches the scream of his racking;

Ropes find the bite and draw on,
And the irony of an inquisitor
Bent confidential to his ear,
Pleads him to yield up the bound fire of his soul

Which he cannot trade.
Until the slow tearing
Wrenches the sin from his marrow
And mangles out his testimony.

Listen.
In the taut space
Amid two versions of his name
There is scratching.

In the dark vault
A lost hand shrieks,
For even its patronym
Has forsaken it.

It flaps across the page
And each splintered finger gibbers.

A jerking, broken wing,
Fluttering against the wall of the confession –

Guido

Sea Glass

Night Swimming

I have been night swimming
Far out in your eyes,

Searching for the love I cast
Into the long draw of your deep tide.

I have out-swum the safe shallows
To glimpse it,
Like a ring
Dropped into dark water.

A fleeting mackerel shimmer
Of watered silver
Spinning,
Just out of reach.

I have lost myself
In watching your eyes
For the glint of my face.

Living for a look
I drift.

My nights are spent swimming
Out of my depth,
Waiting.

I cannot make the shore.

Path of Glass

The string of lights
That once pearled the shoreline
Is cut down.

And each step crunches
On this path of glass.

No one is to blame.
We were not walking there.
It was an unseen wind.

And here are glittering splinters.
Fragile globe shells,
Littering the promenade.

Did I really make too much
Of the time we gave each other?

Moments constellated against darkness,
Too bright to look at singly
(Because my eyes will water)
Each one separate,
Yet strung together –

Bowls of high fire,
I thought would light my way,
That were,
After all,

Just glass.

Shoreline Pompeii

It was early.
I found two casts
In the drying sand –
Where they had lain.

I traced my hand-shadow above them.
The round scoop of her hip,
Against the furrow
Of his straight side.

Here the forms were blurred,
Rumoured with their shifting
And coiling.

A trail of her foot down his leg.
A flicker of his fingers along her back.

I left them
As the tide came,
Chill and drinking
The luxury of their love.

Half closed eyes
Glinting.
Salt on lips –

The promises ... the promises.

Sea Glass

I hold it to the sun –
This gasp of blue,
This frost-pale
Sea glass.

An eager wind
Flurries in ribbons
Along my lips

As your fingers did
When the morning came through your hair

And I was lost
Amid gull's tart cries
Falling in curls –
As lemon peel
On the shingle.

It wets my palm –
This long-ground,
Tide-burred lapis.

It burns on its edges
In glacial flashes

And fits cool under my tongue
Like you have placed it there.

Linen

Here is a bolt of frayed linen.
Such a scrap as you might find
Piled in the booth
Of a dusty bazaar.

It will not dazzle
When thrown up at the sky.

It will not catch the sun in its folds
And pour like silk
Through the merchant's fingers
Into slick patterned stories.

No.
These coarse woven slubs,
Like old mistakes,
Are a natural part of the fabric.

So hold the colours,
The blue and purple
Against your skin.

And I will favour you
When you walk.

And I will lay in whispers
Against your curves.

Like this linen.

Budapest – Fin de Siècle

Over every arch
Cool stone women
Dripped in perfect eliption
Like a row of sleeping tears –

Almost as if they had been waiting
For the oval blue of your eyes.
Or for you to say the magic word.

And Lechner's blunt carvings –
Stern Hun fathers
In Magyar moustaches
Looked down
Like they had just uttered thunder

Then held their breath,
Watching,

As you stood before the Luxus Department Store
And drew your finger across
The high contours,
Sinuous, unlocking.

Then the city opened to your glamour.

In late summer rain
Its lacings wound about your curves,

And I listened
As a thousand watered whispers
Accompanied our wandering,
Fading and rising,
In never finished cycles.

since childhood
violence _ long
in poems that themselves
? refuse to sing or drift
— The Frugs